Fifteenth Episcopal District
African Methodist
Episcopal Church

Rev. Dr. Jessica Kendall Ingram
Supervisor of Missions

16250 Northland Drive
Suite LL16
Southfield, MI 48075

Tel: (248) 569-1550
Fax: (248) 569-2102
E-mail: journeyministries@aol.com

THE JOURNEY INWARD
A Guide To Prayer And Reflection

Jessica Kendall Ingram

Journey Press
Detroit, Michigan

THE JOURNEY INWARD
A Guide To Prayer and Reflection
Copyright 1996 by Journey Press

Library of Congress Cataloging-in-Publication Data Ingram, Jessica.

The Journey Inward: A Guide To Prayer And Reflection

LCCN 96-94264

ISBN 0-9662962-0-6

Cover designed by Elena Farmer

Scriptures are from the New International Version and King James Version translation.

Printed in the United States of America

Dedicated to "Mommie and Daddy"
who started me on this journey

TABLE OF CONTENTS

ACKNOWLEDGMENTS

We never make a journey alone. As we travel we encounter those who give the inspiration, direction, and assistance that we need to stay on the journey. As I have responded to an inner hunger to have a closer walk with God, I have discovered new gifts in me. One of the gifts is the ability to express my thoughts on the written page. Because I have never considered myself to be a writer, I needed and received constant encouragement and support. With deep gratitude I acknowledge those who gave me just what I needed:

My husband — Gregory Ingram, who continuously told me that I could do it!

My daughter — Jennifer, who waited patiently as I spent hours writing at my desk.

My immediate family — (mother) Samantha, Charles, Jean, and Steven, who have always believed in me.

My in-laws — John, Ilene, and Brenda, who constantly gave me words of encouragement.

My church family at Oak Grove A.M.E., who read my weekly reflections in the church bulletin and told me that I must put them in a book.

My ministerial staff - who helped in the research of the scriptures.

My friend, Renetha Weems-Espinso, Ph.D., who critiqued my work and gave me much needed insight.

Additionally I am grateful to Dee Haynes for proofreading the book; Crystal Simmons for typing my work; and to Elena Farmer for the cover design and format.

Most of all, I acknowledge and give honor and glory to God for entrusting this gift to me.

INTRODUCTION

There was no crisis in my life; I was not in the midst of a difficult situation or some deep valley experience. I simply had an inner hunger to want to know more about God. There was a desire developing inside me that was not being satisfied by the outward experience in which I engaged. I was a regular worshipper, extremely active in the church, and I said my prayers, but there was an empty place inside me.

I can't remember the exact day, but one morning in the spring of 1982, I found myself waking up early, going to my favorite living room chair, and sitting there for a good while. I usually spend a few minutes just being quiet because it helped to clear my mind. I would then read from a meditation book, write in my personal journal, read some biblical scriptures, and spend time in prayer. I didn't realize it then, but now I know that I was starting "The Journey Inward."

Since that moment in 1982, I have stayed on the journey. My quiet time increased from 10-15 minutes to one hour. I began to accumulate a variety of meditation books. Journal writing became a daily ritual for me. The scriptures came alive as I read them in the context of a particular spiritual emphasis. Through the years I felt myself becoming increasingly more intimate with God. If I missed my quiet time, I felt off-balanced. I needed to stay on the journey each day. Spending time in the presence of the Lord on a daily basis has made me aware of the undeveloped possibilities in my life. Through prayer and meditation I came to know that *spirituality* is my passion in the ministry.

When I entered the doctoral program at the United Seminary in Dayton, Ohio, my project work focused on prayer. My thesis was entitled, "A Journey In The Experience Of Prayer." My desire was to help others to have an experience similar to mine. I taught lay people how to become spiritual companions and they, in turn, facilitated spiritual formation groups where they guided others through their personal prayer journeys.

After I completed my doctoral work, I wanted to continue writing about the inner dynamics of prayer. So each week I would write a page in our church bulletin entitled, "The Inward Journey." My purpose was not to teach people how to pray, but to help them to understand the "experience of prayer." I chose different themes and developed them. The members of the church loved them so much that they began to encourage me to put the reflections in a book.

The *Journey Inward* is a labor of love for God's people. It is my desire that as you read and experience the journey, you will develop an intimate relationship with God and fulfill your inner longings, which in turn will make a difference in your outward circumstances. Be blessed as you travel.

Rev. Jessica Ingram
April 1996

How To Take The Journey Inward

The Journey Inward is designed to introduce a different theme for each month in the year. Each time you explore the designated theme, something new and exciting will be revealed unto you. The following format will guide you during your quiet time.

I. Moments of Centering

It is important for you to establish a place where you can go to on a regular basis to read your Journey Inward. It should be a place that is comfortable and situated away from distractions (e.g., television, telephones, other people, etc.). Have all your journey materials available, such as your Bible, personal journal, the Journey Inward, and a pen/pencil. In addition, you may listen to a meditation tape if it is not a distraction to you.

Decide whether morning or evening is the best time to spend in your communion with God. Whichever you choose, be consistent. I suggest that you start out with a minimum of 15 to 30 minutes each day devoted to your quiet time. As you progress and become more comfortable and familiar with this time, you may find that the time allotted will increase and vary in length.

When you are ready to start your quiet time, go to your designated place and spend a few moments getting centered. Sit quietly and allow yourself to enjoy the silence for several minutes. Start your meditation tape, if desired. Close your eyes and place your hands, palms up, on your lap. Relax your mind and body. Try to empty your mind of distracting thoughts.

When you feel that you are ready to begin your journey, take note of the theme for the month. Think on it for a few moments. The theme is designed to develop and enhance your inner thoughts concerning prayer. So prepare to explore your feelings on the subject.

II. Prayer

The "Dear God" prayer will assist you in centering your thoughts on the monthly theme. It is a prayer that places you in the presence of the Lord and helps you to present your honest thoughts to God. Pray it on a daily basis. Add your own thoughts as you desire.

III. Journey Scriptures

These scriptures amplify the theme for the month. As you read them, ask yourself: "What is God saying to me in this passage? How can I apply it to my daily life?"

I suggest that you choose a scripture passage and read it each day for a week. Familiarize yourself with it and allow it to become real to you. Use your journal to take note of your feelings, any questions you may have, and any affirmations or directions you may receive.

IV. Journey Reflections

There are four reflections each month — one for each week. Each reflection is designed to elaborate on the theme of the month. Spend some time with the reflection. Read it thoroughly, several times a week. Interact with it. Read slowly, reflectively, and prayerfully.

Ask yourself: What is God saying to me through this word? How can I respond to it? How does it help to develop my understanding of prayer? How does it increase my spiritual awareness? What revelations did I receive? What questions do I have?

V. Journal Writing

Purchase a notebook or journal to be used specifically for writing your personal thoughts and feelings. As you read the scriptures and reflections, and engage in your time of prayer, you will have many thoughts, directions, and questions. Write them down. Write what God says to you and what you need to say to God.

These notes will become your permanent record. You can refer back to them to see your progress and discover new strengths.

Keep your journal in a secure place because these are your private thoughts.

VI. Prayer for the Journey

End your quiet time with prayer. Speak prayers of adoration, thanksgiving, petition, intercession, and surrender.

The moments of centering, the "Dear God" prayer, the scripture reading, the journey reflections, and the journal writing, all contribute to your prayer experience. They become the substance of your praying. Allow your prayer to be a continuation of your quiet time experience.

January

The Journey Inward

"But his delight is in the law of the Lord,
and on His law he meditates day and
night."

Psalm 1:2 (NIV)

I. JOURNEY INWARD

Moments of Centering

Prayer

Dear God,

I cannot make this inward journey by myself. Be thou present with me every step of the way. Help me to listen to your voice and to follow your directions. When I refuse to see what you reveal to me about myself, gently touch me with your Holy Spirit. And when on this journey my soul grows weary, refresh me with your presence. I am determined. Amen.

Journey Scriptures

Journey Reflections

But his delight is in the Law of the Lord and on it he meditates day and night

Deuteronomy 4: 1-7 *follow the commands of God*

Psalm 1

Psalm 42 *as the deer pants for streams of water so my heart pants for you O GOD*

Jeremiah 30:1-2

St. Matthew 6:1-6 *Do Not Worry*

The Inward Journey

Desire

Thinking About God

Journaling As You Travel

Journal Writing

Write your thoughts about making the journey. Look inward and allow your writings to reflect where you are right now.

Prayer for the Journey

Thank you God for these precious moments. I have felt your presence. I am ready to make the journey. Amen.

Jeremiah 30:1-2 The Lord says: Write in a book all the Words I have Spoken to you.

THE JOURNEY INWARD

The journey inward is one that is paradoxical in nature, for as soon as you feel that you have arrived, you will immediately realize that you still have a long way to go. Do not become discouraged. Stay on the journey. There is an uncertain and nebulous dimension to this inward experience. As you travel, you will experience both times of waning and waxing of confidence, and periods of total confusion interspersed with moments of incredibly clear understanding. You will find that it is not wise to think about where you are on the journey or how far you have come; instead, it will be better to think in terms of your inner transformation and the change in your relationship with God.

This inward journey is for those who have become tired of living in a place that does not yield satisfying results. Some have found that place to be oppressive and feel compelled to leave! The decision to travel, to make the journey, will catapult you on a road that leads to a new, spiritual perspective of life. You may not know all of the requirements, but what you do know is that you must leave from where you are. I will tell you that you must travel light. You will have to constantly strip yourself of excess baggage.

We are pilgrims trying to make Heaven our home. It is natural for us to make the journey because within each of us is what the mystics call "the homing instinct." The late Howard Thurman said, "there is a roaming with a hungry heart that is the essential nature of humans." It is the divine discontent of the heart, this sense of restlessness, that compels us to become pilgrim travelers. Unless we make the journey home to God, we remain as exiles and aliens, even to ourselves. The person who makes the journey does not enter into a new land. And there the journey continues. Relax and experience the journey.

DESIRE

About 12 years ago, I began to experience a restlessness, a thirsting in my soul. As I sought to satisfy this longing, this thirsting, I came to understand that my spirit was desiring intimacy with God. It was revealed to me that this intimacy could be experienced not through the "work" that I was doing in the church, but would come only by my taking a journey in prayer. I decided to make the journey.

As I sojourned, I began to pay more attention to what I was experiencing during my prayer time. As I prayed, I noticed that sometimes I felt close to God and had a clear vision of God directing, instructing, and guiding me. At other times, no matter how long and how hard I prayed, I felt nothing, heard nothing, and experienced nothing. As I continued the journey, I repeatedly heard the words, "be still and know that I am God" (Psalms 46:10). My place of stillness became a chair in my living room. In the midst of turmoil, I found rest in that quiet place. There I sat and allowed myself to be filled with the presence of God. The hunger, the thirsting, the desire in my soul was satisfied.

In that quiet place, I have experienced a deepening acquaintance with God. I have learned to strip away the fear, mistrust, and pain that had encased my heart. My years of contemplating God have affirmed that He is closer to me than I realized. On this journey, I have explored God's path with a desire to live a life that is consumed with God. That desire has allowed me to express my innermost self to God, to allow Him to be the source of my transformation and the reason that I am determined to make this journey. I have learned that God will give you the desires of your heart.

THINKING ABOUT GOD

I find that when I am intentional about establishing a time to be quiet before God, disciplining myself to sit in a quiet place, taking some moments to focus my wandering mind and centering on God, I am then able to "think" more clearly about Him. Early in the journey my prayer experience focused mostly on my own little world, but as I continued the journey I found myself thinking more about "God's world." I began to meditate more on God's word and less on my worries. I had journeyed to a place called "contemplative prayer."

It is a different place. My pilgrimage to this new dimension of prayer has not been easy for me. I found that the contemplative prayer experience is made up of times of great and conscious closeness to God. When my prayers make such surrenders, prayer comes easily. And yet, there are times when I feel as though I am a pilgrim just stumbling along the way; and I think of traveling back to the prayer place that is more familiar and less difficult for me. In this new place of prayer, I've tried, I've failed, and I have conveniently forgotten to pray at times. I asked for, and received, forgiveness. I tried and I failed again. But, in spite of the periods of darkness and failure, I continued the journey and I moved closer to God. I found that it is never good to think about where I am as I journey in prayer, rather it is enough to know that I am moving closer to God. During my time of prayer, if God chooses to reveal a dimension of His nature, I rest in the awareness and just "think" about Him for awhile. As I begin to think more about God, my perspective on life begins to change.

Contemplative prayer has enabled me to see my reality in relationship to God. My traveling has become less cumbersome because I am getting more familiar with my eternal travel companion. I like thinking about God. When I do so, I find that my spirit is renewed and refreshed, and I gain the strength to stay on the journey!

Journaling As You Travel

One day I was on my knees in prayer when I felt the presence of God. God reminded me of a promise He had given to me several years ago. Because I had written the words of the promise in my journal, I was able to go back, read, and reclaim the promise. Keeping a journal has enabled me to have a written record of what God is doing in my life and my responses to Him. Keeping a journal is essential on the journey. It is not simply a travel log.

The spiritual discipline of journaling moves beyond mere descriptions of the events on life's road, but instead it provides a place to identify and evaluate the pace of our traveling. Every now and then, I go back and re-read some of my journals. Sometimes I find that I am stuck at the same place — still wrestling with some of the same issues, still asking God the same questions. Other times as I read, I marvel at just how far I have come on this journey. Keeping a journal enables me to stay focused while I travel.

As I sit in my quiet place with my journal, I am able to be my true self before God. Keeping a journal is an act of being real; it is a place where I can be my true self, much like David. Essentially, the Psalms are a record of David's journey and we find that as David wrote down his thoughts, he did not edit them, he was real with God. He wrote about his thanksgiving and he also wrote about his dismay from not hearing from God. He wrote about his spiritual progress, and he also wrote about his stumbling along the way. He recorded his awareness that he should not do evil to his enemy, and he also desired for God to "get them." Keeping a journal kept David honest before God.

Within the realm of our relationship with God there are times when prayer and meditation are beyond our grasp, but the act of gripping a pen seems just right. Sometimes when we just can't pray, writing allows us to still communicate with God. Forming letters across the blank pages provides legible proof of our desire to still make the journey with God. It is there for God and for us to see. Writing helps to get the confusion out. Once we write it down, a release comes. We can then ask God to reorganize all of our disorder into peace and purpose. In that writing space, we develop an "honest" relationship with God. As we write, God continues to give us traveling instructions.

THE JOURNEY INWARD

Journey Thoughts

_____

_____

_____

_____

_____

_____

_____

_____

February

THE DIVINE ENCOUNTER

"In the year that King Uzziah died, I saw
the Lord seated on a throne, high and
exalted, and the train of his robe filled
the temple."

Isaiah 6:1 (NIV)

II. The Divine Encounter

Moments of Centering

Prayer

Dear God,

I cannot begin this day without spending time in your presence. I cannot rush to be with you and quickly move away. I cannot come to the prayer place and not be ready to encounter you. I command my spirit to receive what you will give to me.   Amen.

Journey Scriptures

God talks to Moses
The Burning Bush
About freeing his people
from the Egyptians
I am who I am
(the Israelites are his
people)

Exodus 3:1-8
Isaiah 6:1-8 *and I said, Here*
am I Lord, Send Me
Acts 4:23-31 *Peter + John got*
caught performing
I Chronicles 10:14 *Miracles in Jesus Name*
Judges 6:11-16 *and were asked to stop the miracles*
but could not it in obedience to God

Journey Reflections

On Preparing to Experience God
The Hard Work of Prayer
Prayer- A Meeting Place
Pray Without Ceasing

Journal Writing

As you encounter God, write in your journal what God says to you. Write down how you felt when you were touched by God.

Prayer for the Journey

God, no longer am I afraid to encounter you. In my place of prayer, I have learned to seek your touch. Thank you for touching me with your hand of divine transformation. Amen.

I Chronicles 10:14 The Lord Put Saul to death because he did not Keep the word of the lord, + even consulted a Medium. His Kingdom was turned over to david.

Judges 6:11-16 Gideon was ordered to sack Israel Gideon was worried because he had the weakest clan (but again) the lord replied I am with you.

10

On Preparing to Experience God

Prayer is a place of divine encounter with God. The encounter varies; sometimes it is a confrontation and sometimes it is a sense of presence. It is the coming face to face with a God who is now very near. In that moment, there are not questions. Without asking, we know and we say "surely the presence of the Lord is in this place."

We cannot make God come and yet we must be prepared for His coming. In other words, we all experience times in prayer where no matter how long we have prayed, we get up feeling as though we've just been talking to ourselves. There was no experience of encountering God. If we are not in the habit of praying, we will not know when God's presence is manifest to us. Therefore, men and women "ought to always pray."

Prayer is the place of experiencing God. It is the method by which we make our way to the temple of quiet within our own spirit and the activity of our spirit within ourselves. Prayer is not only the participation in communication with God, it is the "readying" of the spirit for itself and for the experience.

In such "readying," a quiet place is very important. God will not compete with the many noises in our lives. If we want to experience God, we must choose to get quiet and remove the noise. We must turn inward, away from the things that divide and scatter our thoughts and our spirit.

Be patient, something will happen. God will come. When we practice the discipline of being present to God—that is to have a quiet place and an appointed time of being there (with the necessary aids to help us be quiet - the bible, our journals, meditation books)—a strange thing happens. The initiative slips out of our hands and into the hands of God. The self moves toward God. We experience a fundamental stirring that may challenge us, but we don't resist it for we know that "it" is God. We are stimulated, inspired, convicted, renewed, and filled. All of this, however, takes place in a frame of reference that is completely permissive.

Prepare to experience God today. Go to your quiet place and wait for God's coming.

THE HARD WORK OF PRAYER

I have been a student of prayer for the past 16 years of my life. That is to say, I have purposed in my mind and heart to spend time on my knees each day with God. I guess one could say that when it comes to prayer, I am a spiritually disciplined person. And yet with all of my years of praying, I don't feel that I have mastered the art of prayer. Often, I feel that I am starting from the beginning. Prayer is hard work!

The longevity of our years of praying does not guarantee what will happen during our prayer time. Why? I suggest it is because there are always new dimensions of God and for each divine revelation, God comes to us in new ways. We can never become totally familiar with God. God is full of surprises. Sometimes when we kneel to pray, we immediately feel God's presence. It is a touching of the divine. Then there are times when no matter how long we stay on our knees, nothing happens. Absolutely nothing. The temptation is to stop praying.

Presently, I am in a strange place in my prayer life. I can't seem to get settled. I want to stop talking so much and listen, but that's hard because there is so much I want to say. I want to quiet my spirit, but "things" agitate and distract me. I get unfocused. I begin by praying for one thing and before I can pray it through, 52 other things have crowded my mind. It is a frustrating time. Theoretically I know what to do, but it is not being manifested in my prayer experience. I come away from the prayer moment virtually drained. Prayer is hard work and yet I know that I can't stop praying.

Yes, even when it is difficult, boring, and disappointing, I must keep praying. I have come to understand that no matter how jumbled my thoughts or how disoriented I am, every time I come before God, God honors those moments. Although I don't always come away feeling that I have touched God, I have come to know that the efficacy of prayer is not based upon what I feel, but what I know. I know that God is present and hears my every prayer, even the mixed up ones. Although I can't always hear what God is saying and I don't always get an immediate answer, I know that if I keep working at prayer, God will come.

PRAYER - A MEETING PLACE

Personal prayer is the meeting place between the Eternal One and me. That is why I believe in personal prayer and every day I wait for him in my special place. To pray means to wait for the God who comes. Every prayer-filled day means a meeting with the God who comes; every night that we faithfully put ourselves at His disposal becomes full of His presence. His coming and His presence are not only the result of our waiting or a prize for our efforts, they are His decision based on His love freely poured out.

His coming is bound to His promise, not to our works or virtue. We have not earned the meeting with God because we have served Him faithfully or because we have heaped up such a pile of virtue as to shine before Heaven. God is thrust onward by His love, not attracted by our works. God comes even in moments when we have done everything wrong, when we have done nothing, and when we have sinned. God comes.

The point is, God meets us in the place of prayer not based upon who we are and what we have done. We don't earn God's presence because we have been good, and God doesn't withhold His presence because we have not been so good. When God chooses to meet us at the place of prayer, it is a "graced moment." Our place of prayer is then transformed into Holy Ground where we encounter the great "I AM." It becomes the meeting place of our healing, our salvation, our calling, and our hope.

When we pause daily on this journey to pray, we receive the divine initiative to keep traveling. Once we experience the presence of God, "we feel like going on" and we are able to say "surely the presence of the Lord is in this place."

God is the One who meets us at the place of prayer!

PRAY WITHOUT CEASING

The questions, "How long should I pray, where should I pray, and when should I pray?" are often asked by those who are on the journey. During a time of meditation, I came across the following words. I share them with you, my fellow travellers, because I believe that they are essential for your journey.

"The bible does not prescribe the time or length of prayer, but it does offer guidelines. In Psalm 88, prayer is offered early in the morning (verse 13) and in Psalm 55, prayers are said morning, noon and evening (verse 17). The author of Psalm 119 advocates prayer seven times a day (verse 164). Daniel knelt for devotions three times a day (Daniel 6:10). Jesus prayed before sunrise (Mark 1:35) and in the evening when the day's work was over (Mark 6:46). Peter prayed at the third, sixth and ninth hours.

Martin Luther King suggested that prayer should be "the first business of the morning and the last at night." He suggested that we "cultivate the habit of falling asleep with the Lord's Prayer on your lips every evening when you go to bed and again when you get up. And, if the occasion, place and time permit, pray before you do anything else." Calvin suggests that we offer prayer "when we arise in the morning, before we begin daily work, when we sit down to a meal, where by God's blessing we have eaten, and when we are getting ready to retire."

On this journey we are not bound to ritual laws that regulate the preparation of prayer, and we are not bound to set times of prayer. Yet, there are times that are more appropriate for prayer than others such as: the gathering together for worship, the hours before work and bedtime, the time right before meals, and when we need to remind ourselves of the goodness of God. A Christian should feel free to pray anywhere, anytime in the midst of daily work, as well as in the solitude of his/her room in the early morning or late evening.

How long should you pray? The answer comes when you decide how long you would like to be with Jesus. When should you pray? The answer depends upon when you need the Lord. Where should you pray? The answer is "wherever you take the Lord." I would encourage you to adhere to the words of Paul who tells us "to pray without ceasing."

THE DIVINE ENCOUNTER

Journey Thoughts

_____

_____

_____

_____

_____

_____

_____

_____

March

CROSSING THE KIDRON

"When He had finished praying, Jesus left with His disciples and crossed the Kidron Valley. On the other side there was an olive grove, and He and His disciples went into it."

St. John 18:1 (NIV)

III. CROSSING THE KIDRON

Moments of Centering

Prayer

Dear God,

During these days of Lent, I look to you for guidance. This is a time in which I want to be spiritually in tune to what it means to be a follower of Christ. Remove the veil from my eyes so that I might see Him clearly. Implant in me a holy resolve to be like Jesus. Teach me to take up my cross and follow Him. Amen.

Journey Scriptures	Journey Reflections
Genesis 28:10-17	A Letter to Jesus
Deuteronomy 6:10-19	Have You Got Good Religion?
Psalm 78:52-55	Crossing the Kidron
St. John 18:1-11	On The Other Side
Hebrews 3:6-19	

Handwritten notes: Jacob had a dream of a stair way that reached heaven →

I am with you and will watch over you wherever you go

Love the Lord you God... Do not so test the Lord who brought you out of Egypt out of the land of slavery

He guided them safely so they were not afraid

Moses is less than → Jesus
Moses was a servant Jesus is a Son
a warning against Disbelieving

Journal Writing

Write words that articulate your struggles during this Lenten season. Refer to them often. Record what keeps you from crossing the Kidron Valley.

Prayer for the Journey

God, I believe that I am ready to cross over now. When I become fearful, remind me that Jesus crossed the Kidron Valley just for me. Amen.

St. John 18:1-11 Jesus is arrested

A Letter To Jesus

Dear Jesus,

The Lenten season has begun, and I know that it's a time to be with you in a special way. It is a time to pray, fast, and follow you on your way to Jerusalem, to Golgotha, and to the final victory over death. If I can be real with you, I need to tell you that I am still so divided and confused. I want to follow you, but I also want to yield to my own desires and listen to the voices that speak about prestige, success, pleasure, power, and influence. Help me Jesus to become deaf to these voices and more attentive to yours.

I know that Lent is going to be a very hard time for me. The choice for your way has been made every moment of my life. I have to choose thoughts that are your thoughts, words that are your words, and actions that are your actions. There are not times or places without choices, and I know how deeply I resist choosing you.

Please Lord, be with me at every moment and in every place. Give me the strength and the courage to live this season faithfully so that when Easter comes, I will be able to taste with joy the new life that you have prepared for me. Amen.

Dear Child,

I have heard your prayer and I like your honesty. Yes, this will be a difficult season for you, but you must always remember that even when you are unable to keep your commitment I will still love you. Keep in mind that Jesus, your Savior, is sitting at my right hand talking to me about you. Even at this present moment. The Holy Spirit is preparing ministering angels to strengthen you during your weak moments, and I am rejoicing because you have decided to make the journey. Remember, you can do all things through my son, Jesus, who will give you strength.

With you on this Journey,

God

HAVE YOU GOT GOOD RELIGION?

Religion in its root meaning (re-ligare) means to re-tie, to re-connect to God. It is to bind us again to the source from whom we came and to whom we are on a pilgrimage. The practice of the spiritual disciplines is the way in which we get re-connected to God.

Many people recoil at the word discipline. Very few willingly embrace it. We usually kick, scream, struggle, and resist. Perhaps this is due to a lack of knowledge of what the practice of the spiritual disciplines do for us and our relationship to God. Ultimately, they bring us in the presence of God and usher us into a place of divine intimacy.

To be disciplined is to persist daily in our efforts to know God. Each day we must engage in those experiences that "re-connect" us with God. In the course of any given moment our spirits are broken, assaulted, attacked, strained, or disturbed. When this happens, we often become discouraged, confused, weary, unfocused, and depressed. We begin to feel that we are not in touch with God. God seems to be so far away.

We have entered the Lenten season. It is not a time in which we concentrate on giving up things that we don't need, like smoking and eating too much. Instead, it is a season in which we can "get good religion." The ultimate purpose of Lent is for us to re-establish, or to re-connect, with God. We do so by participating in the practice of spiritual disciplines. We must view the discipline of worship, meditation, study of God's word, prayer, and fasting not as dull work that we resent, but as opportunities to reenforce our connection to God. Spiritual discipline is not a vain effort to save oneself, it is an intelligent application of the spiritual principles that enables us to enter into a life-giving relationship with God.

When Easter Sunday comes, will you be able to say "I've got good religion?" You can, if you purpose in your heart this day that you will persist in practicing the spiritual discipline. Then you will be able to say, "I've got good religion, certainly Lord."

CROSSING THE KIDRON

The Lenten season is a time of decision. It is a season in which we cannot hide from the inescapable reality of facing some hard choices. Will I continue to do it my way or will I yield to God knowing that I will have to make some sacrifices? This is a time of challenge and decision.

The days ahead of us require that we engage in an exacting struggle of the soul. It is a struggle because we have become attached to things, people, places, desires, and ambitions. This is the season of detachment. We struggle because we are not sure that we want to let go. It is an inner struggle that brings us face to face with the questions: "Do I really love God enough to do this? Do I want to make the sacrifice? Do I want to cross over the Kidron?"

What is significant is that when Jesus was entering into His last days of earthly ministry, He prayed to God in earnest. Although He had lived in total obedience, He knew that what awaited Him on the other side of the Kidron would require a new level of sacrifice. Thus, before He crossed over, He prayed.

This geographical location is symbolic of a spiritual truth. The Kidron Valley was east of the city of Jerusalem. The name means dark, not clear, and murky. South of Jerusalem, the Kidron turns into a wilderness and empties into the Dead Sea. There, debris and trash has accumulated. This valley represents the place of confusion and uncertainty in us, the irritation we experience when God is trying to move us into a new realm of the spirit. This valley becomes symbolic of our need to confront the darkness in us, our blind spots, the places where we have refused to see and where, for lack of spiritual nourishment, we are dying from the debris of life that is accumulating in our minds.

There is a danger that confronts us. If we don't make the decision to cross over, if we stay on the other side too long, we will find ourselves emptying into the abyss of "nothingness." To remove the fears, doubts, concerns, and attachments, we must pray. Only prayer gives us the insight, the wisdom, the yielding, and the strength to say yes to God and cross over the Kidron.

ON THE OTHER SIDE

We each have moments when we must make a decision. Decisions require that we release something old and embrace something new. In this position, we are often in a valley that separates us from thinking about it and making that final decision. If we really look at the valley, we see deep, dark places. We're not attracted to what awaits us there, but before we can move to the other side, we must go through it.

Once we decide that what awaits us on the other side is worth the difficulties that we will experience, the valley is no longer a threat to us. To cross the valley, we must say yes to God and no to ourselves. In other words, we must sacrifice.

We fear this word, sacrifice. Sacrifice is difficult because of our attachment, our being accustomed to having a particular thing or experience. We think that the very presence of this thing or experience is satisfying and it gives us a degree of identity. We feel that this thing or experience is ours alone and we do not want to let it go.

We are not always asked to sacrifice something because it is bad or evil, but because it is a hindrance to our moving forward. When we refuse to let go, when we hold on to something that is past its season, when we will not release, then we stay in the valley and miss the next move of God in our lives. There comes a moment when we must decide whether to cross over to the other side.

When we look at the storms, the trials, and the tribulations that we know lie in the valley, we began to hold even tighter to our false securities, inadequate support systems, emotional manipulations, victim mentalities, and childish fears. We must, however, move to the place of determined resolve. We must decide that no matter what confronts us in the valley, we will not return to our old ways. We will detach ourselves, learn to live with a sense of discomfort, and cross over to the other side. Remember, sacrifice always makes us uneasy for a season.

When we resolve in our spirit to willingly go over to the other side, then we begin to move without looking to the right or left. Those things that were once so important become a fading memory.

It will take a lot of hard work to get to the other side. You will experience moments of doubt. The times of sorrow and grief may come, but when you make that decision to go, nothing can turn you around. Once you arrive, your song will be:

(How I got over, how I got over, my soul looks back and wonders, how I got over!)

CROSSING THE KIDRON

_____

_____

_____

_____

_____

_____

_____

_____

_____

April

GOING THROUGH

"Blessed are those whose strength is in you, who have set their hearts on pilgrimage. As they pass through the Valley of Baca, they make it a place of springs; the autumn rain also cover it with pools. They go from strength to strength, till each appears before God in Zion."

Psalm 84: 5-7 (NIV)

IV. Going Through

Moments of Centering

Prayer

Dear God,

I will lift up mine eyes unto the hills from whence cometh my help. Lately I have found myself to be in a low place and yet my spirit is not confined to this valley. I look to you God, because I know that only you can see me through. Amen.

Journey Scriptures

Put your Hope In God
Even the sparrow has found a home and the swallow a Nest for herself where she may house her young a place Near your altar

— Psalm 43:1-5
Psalm 84:1-7
St. Matthew 11:25-30
Hebrews 10:32-39
Romans 8:18-39

Come to me, all you who are weary and burdened and I will Give you rest

Journey Reflections

Journey Through the Valley of Baca
Praying Through Confusion
Prayer Brings It Together
Getting Through

Journal Writing

We experience different feelings when we are going through. Be honest when recording your thoughts, whatever they may be. Allow yourself to sit with them for awhile.

Prayer for the Journey

God, the valley doesn't seem so low now. My time with you has helped me to see how to go through. Prayer has been my place of travel. Amen.

Psalm 84:1-7
As they pass through the Valley of Baca, they make it a place of Springs Bac Means Weep Baca was a Valley of weeping then, When you come to this Valley stay on course instead of losing your direction. God is teaching us even in the Valley of Baca Let Him plan the course

JOURNEY THROUGH THE VALLEY OF BACA

As we make the inward journey, so often we are too full of what we think should be happening to us to notice what God is actually teaching us. If you have decided to make the journey, you will pass through the Valley of Baca. Baca was a valley containing trees that exuded resin or gum. The Hebrew term "baka" is related to "weep" hence, Baca was a valley of weeping trees. Often, when we come to this valley — to places that cause us to weep — we tend to get off course and lose our direction. Instead of concentrating on where we are going, we begin to focus on this momentary delay. We are now no longer traveling forward, but find ourselves becoming frantic and virtually going in circles. Our spiritual compass has gone haywire and we really don't know which way we are going. We must learn to be still long enough to experience what God is teaching us even in the Valley of Baca. Let Him plan the course. We must learn how to get through the valley with a minimum of damage and a maximum of growth.

As you travel and come to Baca, keep your heart set on the pilgrimage — the journey. Remember that Baca is but a stopping place on the way to Jerusalem, which in Hebrew means, "City of Peace and Wholeness." If you keep traveling you will get to Jerusalem, but to get there you must keep meditating, praying, praising, and worshipping the Lord. If you do so, you will gain strength from the journey and one day you will find that you have travelled through the valley.

Praying Through Confusion

Writing this Journey Inward was a serious struggle for me. I tried to put it off until the very last minute. When I started to write, my mind went completely blank, my head began to hurt, and I had mild anxiety attacks. Questions ran rampant through my mind. I asked, "God, what should I write? How should I say it? Will anyone read it? Will it make any sense?" Then I moved into the realm of insecurity and I said to myself, "you know, you really aren't a writer anyway. Who told you that you had something worthwhile to say? You really should try to use bigger words and more descriptive phrases." I searched frantically through my books trying to find just one thought. Discarded pieces of yellow, legal pad paper ended up on the floor around my chair, as I tore up page after page. Writing is hard work! And yet, I knew that I must write!

My struggle to write mirrors our struggle in prayer. Praying is something we need to do, but we don't always feel like doing it. Prayer is not an orderly experience. If we are honest, we would admit that there are times when we don't look forward to it. Nighttime comes and we say we are too exhausted to pray. Morning comes and we say it's too early to pray. Too often we put it off.

There are times we can't think of what to say. We say the same thing over and over again. Surely God wants to hear something different. Our thoughts are chaotic. They don't make sense to us or to God (so we think). We begin to question ourselves. "Who am I to ask anything of God? Does He really want to hear this? Am I worthy of talking to God? Do I really want to hear what God has to say?" All around our prayer place, we toss bits of prayers — ones that we begin to pray and then decided to forget them. But somehow, in spite of all the inner turmoil, we know that we must pray.

Prayer Brings It All Together

Prayer is not an orderly experience. It would be wonderful if during the prayer moments all of our thoughts were neatly arranged and organized. We long for those times when our words just flow. Instead, we find that there are seasons when we don't know what we ought to pray. The trick of the evil spirit is to make us think that the confusion we sometimes experience in prayer determines the effectiveness of our prayers. The evil spirit would have us to believe that our inner turmoil negates God's response to us. When we allow ourselves to believe this deception, we begin to pray less or not at all.

I have refused to yield to the confusion that I encounter when it is time to write. I persevered in spite of all the anxiety, chaos, and disorder in my thoughts. I have found that if I keep working at it, eventually all the pieces come together. And so it is with prayer. We don't always want to pray, but we must pray anyhow! There are times when words fail us — pray anyhow (the spirit makes intercession for us). We begin and we stop, but we must go back and pray again. If we continue to pray, there will come a time in which all of the pieces suddenly fit together. It happens because the effectiveness of prayer is not contingent upon our ability to move smoothly through the prayer moment, instead it has to do with our desire to be in the presence of God. God does not require perfectly organized prayers before He responds. What God does honor is our desire to be with Him and our believing that He can put the pieces together.

GETTING THROUGH

So often we are too full of what we think should be happening to us in our spiritual formation to notice what God is actually teaching us. We must be still enough, simple enough, and humble enough to let God plan the course and use whatever opportunities there may be for our instruction.

Being still is an act of the will that places us in a position to be taught by God. Our culture teaches us that a full agenda each day is evidence of our progress. God teaches us the opposite. Only when we empty ourselves of the busyness and the clutter will we make spiritual progress. What we need is not the so-called deep, mystical experiences, but the simple things like praying often, reading the scripture daily, and worshipping each Sunday. We must realize that without the presence of God in our lives we would be nothing. So we have no cause to be egotistical, puffed up, and arrogant.

Prayer is a place of God's instructing us, but we must not think that as we progress in prayer everything will necessarily become more overtly different. No, what it will become is more simple, more humble, and more actual. This is how we learn to get through situations in our lives. We must learn how not to be swamped by the situations in which we find ourselves. What we learn from the spiritual discipline is how to get through and pass over to the other side.

If, then, we desire a simple test of the quality of our spiritual life, a consideration of the tranquility, gentleness, and strength with which we deal with the circumstances of our outward life will serve us better than anything that is based on false progress, notions, or feeling. Tranquility, gentleness, and strength carry us through the changes of life; its ups and downs, the inequalities, emotional and professional disappointments, the sudden intervention of bad health, and the rising and falling of our religious temperature.

Getting through is more than engaging in positive thoughts. Getting through is to be in prayer without ceasing, leaving the results to God, and releasing ourselves to be alright with God's way and His timing. Getting through means that we stay still long enough and often enough to know that not in the wind or the earthquake, but in the simple, little ways, God is taking care of the matter. Our responsibility is simply to keep living a life in His presence. Our simple prayers get us through.

Going Through

Journey Thoughts

_____

_____

_____

_____

_____

_____

_____

_____

_____

May

PREPARATION FOR PENTECOST

"After they prayed, the place where they
were meeting was shaken."

Acts 4: 31 (NIV)

V. Preparation for Pentecost

Moments of Centering

Prayer

Dear God,

I welcome your Holy Spirit in my life this day. I am in need of your teaching, guidance, correction, and direction. Help me not to draw back when your spirit comes forth. Give me the patience to wait and to know that your Holy Spirit is working in me, both to will and do your good pleasure. Amen.

Journey Scriptures

Psalm 25:4-5
II Chronicles 7:11-14
Acts 1:1-4
Acts 4:23-31
James 5:13-18

Journey Reflections

Prayer - Preparation for Pentecost
Prayer Changes You
Praying for the Change
Prayer - A Pentecostal Experience

Journal Writing

To pray is to change. Write about your change.

Prayer

Dear God,

Pentecost is real to me. As I waited for you in prayer, you came, and your coming has brought new awareness and divine desires in my life. Thank you God. Amen.

PRAYER - PREPARATION FOR PENTECOST

If you want to receive the promise of God, you must learn to stay in Jerusalem and wait. When Jesus spoke the words in Acts 1:4, He was essentially telling them to pray. Prayer is a place of staying and waiting. In order to pray, we must learn how to remain in the appointed place until we receive the release to leave. To wait in that place is more than the act of inactivity.

Jesus told the disciples to stay in Jerusalem. For the disciples, Jerusalem was not a comfortable place. It was in this city that the demons in them had come forth. Jerusalem was the city where they had lied, betrayed, and deserted Jesus. To stay in Jerusalem was to remain in the very place where they had "messed up." To remain in this city meant they would have to confront their demons.

When we pray, we too must come to grips with who we are and the things that we have done to Jesus. To pray is to stay in Jerusalem. It is the experience of being still long enough for God to reveal to us our "inner self." Often when we pray, we leave prematurely because it is difficult for us to face our true selves.

It would have been easy for the disciples to leave, but the command was to wait. Jesus was not instructing them to simply stay in that upper room until something happened, instead he was telling them to commune with God. Waiting on God is the experience of being connected to Him. It involves the conscious and intentional act of being in God's presence. If we are to experience a transition in our lives, we must learn to wait in the place that has been designated by God. The length of our stay is determined by God, not us. As we wait and pray, God will send the Holy Spirit to fill us. When we leave, we will know that we have been in the presence of God. We will know that we are not the same.

PRAYER CHANGES YOU

When the day of Pentecost came, the disciples were changed. It happened because for ten days they were assembled in a room where they prayed. (They all joined together constantly in prayer...Acts 1:14.) Prior to that day, the disciples were a group of people who were weak-minded, inconsistent, easily persuaded, liars, and betrayers. Their insight into the work of Jesus was limited, their over-sized egos interfered with the humility that was needed to follow Jesus, and they were blinded by their natural way of seeing things. They needed to be changed.

To pray is to change. Prayer changes us. The primary purpose of prayer is to bring such a life of communion with God, that by the power of the spirit we are increasingly conformed to the image of Jesus.

Prayer will change us not based upon our own efforts, but on the work of God, Jesus, and the Holy Spirit. The gift of salvation (not our works), places us in the position to go boldly before the throne of God. Salvation gives us the right to commune with God. Often when we try to pray, however, we do not know how. But we need not worry, for Romans 8:26-27 tells us that the Spirit helps us in our weakness for we do not know how to pray as we ought, but the Spirit intercedes with sighs too deep for words. God, who searches our hearts, knows what is the mind of the spirit because the Spirit intercedes for us and is lining up our Spirit, our mind, our thoughts, and our ways with the will of God. That is change.

And, it gets even better. The writer to the Hebrews reminds us that Jesus Christ is our High Priest. The function of the High Priest in ancient Israel was to intercede before God on behalf of the people (Hebrew 7-9). This means that when we pray, not only is the Holy Spirit interpreting for us, but Jesus is also interceding for us. He is praying on our behalf. Continual prayer is offered at the throne of God by none other than the Eternal Son. Jesus is praying for our change.

Praying For The Change

Jesus is praying for our change. He is sitting at the right hand of God this very moment interceding in prayer for us. This means that there is not a moment in our day where we are not covered in prayer by the one who knows our every need, our inner-most thoughts, and those places in us that stand in need of conversion.

I remind you again that the work of prayer is not ours alone. Often we feel as though our prayer efforts are futile. We come to the prayer moment with confusion, lack of clarity, stumbling through our words, and a fear of being authentic with God. We can, however, find comfort in knowing that not only is the Holy Spirit and Jesus with us in our feeble efforts of praying, but God is in everlasting communion with Himself through our bumbling prayers. Someone once said, "when we speak to God, it is really the God who lives in us speaking through us to Himself...the dialogue of grace is really the monologue of the divine nature in self-communing love. We pray and yet it is not we who pray, but a Greater One who prays in us."

The spirit that wars against our changing would have us to believe that our prayers for inner change are futile. We pray and then, seemingly, end up doing the same thing we just prayed about not doing. Paul captures our sense of frustration in Romans 7:18-19..."for I have the desire to do what is good, but I cannot carry it out. For what I did is not the good I want to do; nor the evil I do not want to do — this I keep on doing." Paul goes on to ask, "Who will rescue me from this dilemma?"

Thank God, we have found the answer. We have the activity of the everlasting Trinity working on our behalf. God the Holy Spirit is interpreting our sighs and groans before the throne of Heaven. God the Son is interceding on our behalf before the throne of Heaven. And God the Father, who sits upon the throne, is using our prayers to form a perfect soliloquy — God speaking to God. Now with such divine activity we can relax and know that when we pray, our change will come!

PRAYER - A PENTECOSTAL EXPERIENCE

In order to "experience" the presence of the Holy Spirit in our prayer moments, we must learn to invoke His presence. On the day of Pentecost, the disciples did not pray selfish prayers where they concentrated on their fleshly desires and needs. Instead, they prayed prayers of forgiveness, cleansing, and purging. In so doing, their spirits were ready to receive the manifestation of the Holy Spirit. When the day of Pentecost came, they were filled with God's presence because they had prayed. We too can have a pentecostal experience in our time of praying. I suggest that we pray the words of this song:

O SPIRIT of the LIVING GOD

O spirit of the living God
Thou light and fire divine
Descend upon me once more
And make me truly thine.
Fill me with love and joy and power
With righteousness and peace
till Christ shall dwell within my heart
and sin and sorrow cease

Blow, wind of God
Until my mind is free
Burn winged fire! Inspire my lips
With flaming love and zeal
to tell to all thy great news
And to live it as thou has willed.

PREPARATION FOR PENTECOST

Journey Thoughts

_____

_____

_____

_____

_____

_____

_____

_____

_____

June

A Listening Place

"Incline your ear and come to me: hear,
and your soul shall live; and I will make
an everlasting covenant with you, even
the sure mercies of David."

Isaiah 55:3 (KJV)

VI. A Listening Place

Moments of Centering
Prayer

Dear God,

I want to be like Jesus, not only in my works, but in my ability to get by myself and listen to your voice. I am so accustomed to the sounds around me until I am not sure that I can do this. So, I humbly ask you to teach me how to hear.   Amen.

Journey Scriptures

I Samuel 3:1-10
Isaiah 32:9-20
Genesis 32:9-31
St. Mark 1:29-39

Journey Reflections

A Listening Place
The Discipline of Listening
Sit, Listen, and Wait
A New Way of Listening

Journal Writing

Write the words that God has spoken to you. Re-visit them from time to time.

Prayer for the Journey

Dear God,

In the midst of all the noise in my life, I have learned to recognize your voice. The sound is as sweet music to my ear. I will continue to listen.   Amen.

A Listening Place

There comes a time when we must do as Jesus did, leave the crowd and go off to a solitary place. A place where we can listen. Our time alone with God is one of refreshing, renewal, and recommitment. When we spend specific, designated time with God — giving Him our full attention — our souls are reunited with Him and intimacy is established. God sends His ministering angels to us with messages of comfort and affirmation. It becomes our secret place where God speaks to our inner most parts and reveals His thoughts to us. When we care enough to practice the discipline of listening, God honors that place.

We need a place where we can wrestle with God all by ourselves. There comes a time when we must leave family, friends, and possessions and go to that place where we can confront our demons. When God wanted Jacob to listen, He took him across the Jabbok river. Jacob went alone (Genesis 32:22-24) and wrestled with God all night long. He had to rid himself of the many voices within that spoke those things that were contrary to God's will. These voices have occupied a place in us for so long until they will not get up and go of their own free will. A wrestling match must take place. When day break came, Jacob was a different person.

As the spirit of God leads us, we must cross the river Jabbok and go to a solitary place too. There are visions, purposes, missions, and directions that God wants to reveal to us. It will not happen in the midst of the noise and clutter of our lives. We cannot hear God's voice for it is dulled by the many sounds around us. We cross over, not in fear of being alone, but in divine anticipation of what God will speak to us.

For the past 14 years, my listening place has been the brown chair in my living room. Although I have moved at least seven times during those years, my chair has always been the focal point of my time with God. Somehow, each day when I rise and go to there, I feel as though it is just God and me there. God has spoken so much to me. I was not ready for what I heard, but I knew in my spirit that whatever God spoke to me was ultimately for my own good.

A listening place is necessary to the journey. Take the time to create a listening place in your home and each day enjoy the voice of a God who longs to speak to you. It will change your life.

The Discipline Of Listening

A spiritual life without discipline is impossible. Discipline is the other side of discipleship. We cannot call ourselves followers of Christ if we do not practice the spiritual disciplines. Engaging in works without benefit of the disciplines would make us become as "sounding brass and tinkling cymbals."

The practice of a spiritual discipline makes us more sensitive to the small, gentle voice of God. The prophet Elijah did not encounter God in the mighty wind or in the earthquake or in the fire, but in a small voice (I Kings 19:9-13). Through the practice of spiritual disciplines, we become attentive to that small voice and willing to respond when we hear it.

We are surrounded by so much inner and outer noise until it is hard to truly hear God when He is speaking to us. We have often become deaf, unable to know when God calls us and unable to understand in which direction He calls us. Thus, our lives have become absurd. In the word absurd, we find the Latin word surdus, which means "deaf." A spiritual life requires discipline because we need to learn to listen to God who constantly speaks, but whom we seldom hear. When we learn to listen, our lives become obedient ones. The word obedient comes from the Latin word audire, which means "listening." A spiritual discipline is necessary in order to move slowly from an absurd life to an obedient life; from a life filled with noisy worries to a life in which there is some true inner space where we can listen to our God and follow His guidance. Jesus' life was a life of obedience. He was always listening to God, always attentive to his voice, and always alert for His directions. Jesus was "all ears." True prayer involves being all ears for God. The core of all prayer is indeed listening and obediently standing in the presence of God.

Listening is a spiritual discipline. It is the concentrated effort to create some inner and outer space in our lives where this obedience can be practiced. Through the spiritual disciplines, we prevent the world from filling our lives to such an extent that there is no place left to listen.

Today draw nearer to God by practicing the discipline of listening.

Sit, Listen, And Wait

Any serious, daily practice of contemplative prayer will give some taste of the following experience. You sit in prayer and on the surface there is nothing. Yet, as the noise of your next thought falls away, as you allow the silence to deepen around and within you, you discover that you are on the trackless waters on which Jesus bid Peter to walk in order to be united with Him. It is a path in which there is "no light except the one that burns in your heart." You set out to find Him who calls you out of nothingness to union with Himself. You set out knowing that you must find God, yet the first step leaves you lost. An inner wisdom tells you that "to reach Him whom you do not know, you must go by a way you do not know."

Prayer never touches us as long as it remains on the surface of our lives, as long as it is nothing but one more of the ten thousand things that must be done. It is only when prayer becomes "the one thing necessary" that real prayer begins. Prayer begins to take on its full dimensions only when we begin to intuit that the subtle nothingness of prayer is everything. Prayer begins when we go to our place of prayer as to a sacred place.

Prayer is not about our effort as much as it is about God's response. Many of us approach prayer as a task to be accomplished through what we do. We measure the effectiveness of our prayers based on our efforts. We come to the prayer moment with tensions and an expectation of quick results. A small, green apple cannot ripen in one night by tightening all its muscles, squinting its eyes, and tightening its jaw in order to find itself the next morning miraculously large, red, ripe, and juicy beside its small, green counterparts. Like the birth of a baby, or the opening of a rose, the birth of the self takes place in God's time. We must wait for God, we must be aware and we must trust in His hidden action within us.

In the midst of my busy schedule, I decided to go on a two-day private retreat. I was excited about having uninterrupted time to read, reflect, write in my journal, and pray. On the first day, I entered the chapel and after reading some scriptures I began to pray. I was praying real hard telling God everything I could possibly say. While I was going through my litany, I clearly heard God say, "slow down, you are talking too much. I have something to say to you. Stop talking, sit quietly, listen, and wait." Until you do so, you have not prayed.

A New Way Of Praying

Isaac, a Syrian monk of Ninevah, once said, "Those who delight in a multitude of words, even though they say admirable things, are empty within." And so it is with our praying. We come to the prayer moment with a multitude of words. What we speak sounds good, and because of our talking too much, we often come away empty. Contemplative prayer is the one discipline that can free us from our addiction to words and usher us into a place of listening to God. Progress in prayer means progress toward silence. "For God alone my soul waits in silence" (Psalm 62:1). A desert father says, "I have shown you the power of silence, how it thoroughly heals and how fully pleasing it is to God." Know that it is by silence that the saints grew, and it was because of silence that the power of God was known to them.

Contemplation is an attitude of listening awareness; where we are engulfed in the presence of God, where our hearts are strangely warmed, where the core of our being is touched, and where we are transformed. By learning to decrease our words and develop more of a listening mode, we come into a new way of seeing. Our perspective on the whole of life changes, because we now hear life through the voice of God. Contemplation is being a prayer, not just saying one.

In contemplative prayer, we allow ourselves to be acted upon rather than acting as agents. Most likely we bring our own intentions, images, and perception to prayer even when we are interceding for others and giving God praise. At some point in our prayer growth we ought to move beyond our present concepts and images. The act of contemplation is a process of letting go of the familiar. We become too comfortable and too familiar in our praying and never really move to another place on this journey. We like to talk because we know what we want to say to God, but contemplation requires silence so that we hear what God has to say to us. We grow more by listening to what God is saying rather than by hearing ourselves talk all the time in the prayer moment.

To enter into contemplative prayer is a radical act and it is risky. It is to open ourselves to be changed in some way into God's own self. It is a formative life; it changes us and our perceptions. Thus, it is prayer where we allow ourselves to die — continuously. Prayer becomes a place of being stripped over and over again of the comfortable and the familiar, and allowing a reality beyond our own to shape us.

When we posture ourselves to be quiet before God, we come to know Him in different ways. As we make ourselves more available to God, we increase our knowing that God is really with us. We know this not just intellectually, but experientially. Because this kind of praying is a deepening experience, we enter into the deeper places of God. Our deepest aspirations and longings are satisfied, and our emptiness fulfilled.

In our natural life, we have the need to know, control, manage, and manipulate it. Contemplative prayer dismisses such notions. As we consciously open ourselves to God, we find that we cannot control, manipulate, or manage God. Ironically, this is the posture to be assumed if we want to know God. Our not knowing positions us to know. And yet, if we are committed to the process, we experience grace moments when the abundance of God's love overwhelms us and His light shines so brightly until we find ourselves saying, "It is good to be here!"

We live in a season where we are surrounded by things and crowds, yet we are a lonely people. Prayer has a profound effect on our loneliness. It changes loneliness into solitude. Loneliness is an absence and emptiness. Solitude is loneliness transformed in a space that God occupies. The decision to make contemplative prayer a part of our lives, and to move toward a centered life, is a decision to move from loneliness to solitude. It is to decide to choose a life of quality, to decide to choose consistently what is truly to our good and to our true happiness, and to decide to choose to pray in a new way.

A LISTENING PLACE

Journey Thoughts

_____

_____

_____

_____

_____

_____

_____

_____

July

IN THE PURSUIT OF HEALING

"The Lord is close to the brokenhearted
and saves those who are crushed in
spirit."

Psalm 34:18 (NIV)

VII. In The Pursuit Of Healing

Moments of Centering

Prayer

Dear God,

I pray this song to you today.

> *"O thou in whose presence my soul takes delight,*
> *In whom in affliction I call,*
> *My comfort by day, my song by night,*
> *My hope, my salvation, my all."*

It is in your presence alone that I experience the joy and comfort that I need. I thank you for the healing covering that you will give me this day. Amen.

Journey Scriptures	Journey Reflections
Psalm 34:1-18	In The Matter Of Blessings
Psalm 55:1-22	And Yet Will I Rejoice
Habakkuk 3:17-19	Your Faith Makes You Whole
St. Mark 5:21-34	What Becomes of the Brokenhearted
Romans 8:18-39	

Journal Writing

David wrote of his pain. It was a part of his healing process. Write until it hurts and then write until you are healed.

<u>Prayer for the Journey</u>

Dear God,

    I feel better now. Your word has ministered to my hurt. You are close to the brokenhearted. I have felt your presence and I know that I am not alone. Amen.

In The Matter Of Blessing

The writing of our innermost thoughts and praying from the deepest part of our heart, are instruments of our healing. In seasons of brokenness, our healing comes through our willingness to present our wounded selves to a loving and caring God. The process will hurt, but in order to be healed we must touch the place of our pain. This truth became evident to me through a letter shared by a precious gentlemen who, though it caused him discomfort, sat down and wrote his thoughts for me. I share them with you in the hope that they will become instruments of your healing.

Dear Rev. Jessica,

The Lord placed it upon my heart to write this message partly as an instrument for my own healing. This is neither an exercise in form, nor a flirtation with fashion, it is simply one wounded brother's attempt to reach out to Aba Father with a prayer that I may become irresistible to Him.

As I gaze upon the life tree of my own personal experience, I can hardly contain the joy I feel about the wonderful blessings the Lord has bestowed upon me. My wife and three wonderful daughters represent the sweet fruit of this tree. I realize that it will take great effort and consistency to execute the responsibility necessary to make for them a safe and secure home life. I also realize that it is not me who will be the author of the plans which leads us to a place of sanctuary. It is the Lord. So, I seek His face, but my effort to seek Him in prayer have been inconsistent. In fact, if the truth be told, I generally only seek Him in times of trouble and despair. When the ocean is calm and the boat is taking in no water, my praise and prayer seldom reaches those deeper cords. The bellow of my prayer is more like a fainting wisp than a driving wind and the tenor of my prayer loses its brightness. I've often wondered why I tend to give less to the one who gives all. I pray for answers to this question and God has come forward with revelation. It's

in the brokenness. It's in the woundedness. The answers resides in those places where most of us would rather not go. We hide these places from others, ourselves and we attempt to hide them from God. We pretend that they don't exist and somehow they will magically go away. But, like the morning dew on our fields of dreams, the woundedness and brokenness persist. They cloud our ability to truly establish a close personal relationship with God. I have concluded that it is time to walk with Jesus on another level.

I can no longer be satisfied with what I know are fetid offerings, half-baked prayers and postured praise. Lying prostrate before the Lord and confessing my woundedness and brokenness is essential. I must be broken to heal the brokenness and wounded to heal the woundedness. There is a breaking and a wounding in pursuit of that healing place and I accept this as part of the journey.

AND YET I WILL REJOICE

If you do not have a prayer life, you will not be able to rejoice! To rejoice is not an experience that emanates from a life of orderly circumstances. It is a spiritual state that is obtained by those whose joy is not confined to their neatly packaged experiences. "And yet," means that in spite of what I am going through, I can ascertain the fullness of joy.

There are times in the life of all Christian believers when the fig tree simply does not blossom. Times when, in spite of all of our labor, we seemingly produce nothing. These are moments in which we begin to despair and find ourselves in a posture of gloom. Our journey is filled with untimely disappointments that can, and will, cause us to doubt ourselves and question God. We find that these unexplainable, unwanted interruptions in our lives throw us off balance. They bruise our already fragile hearts and disorient us. We are filled with the temptation to lose heart and to give up. It is these moments that are the ingredients for prayer. The efficacy of prayer is found in our having the need to pray.

When the barren places of this life catapult us to confusion and anguish, we need to pray. We now have an urgent need to commune with God, who has been patiently waiting to hear from us. Be encouraged God is plenteous in mercy and abounds in love for us, such that even though we come to Him out of the desperation of our situation, He is always ready to receive our prayer petitions. As you relax in God's comforting presence, you will find that what once had you living in a state of turmoil begins to yield to the calming presence of an Almighty God.

You can rejoice always, if you learn to pray anyhow. We speak not of some self-induced psychological escape from our present realities, but of a spiritual truth that does not allow our rejoicing to emanate from what we have, but it comes in knowing who has us!

YOUR FAITH MAKES YOU WHOLE

Brokenness is an inevitable condition of this life. None of us live without experiencing some season(s) where we find ourselves struggling to put the pieces of our shattered dreams together. There are unwelcome intrusions that cause a disruption in our journey. We must take time to attend to our wounds. Like the woman with the issue of blood, we try in many ways to mend our condition, only to find that we really are no better, and perhaps worse. We are still living in a place called broken. When we come to realize that our healing will not be found in self-made remedies, then and only then will our healing begin!

We are the product of a culture that is addicted to quick fixes. Thus, we try those "things" that we think will give us some immediate relief. After all, who wants to live in pain for an extended period of time? So we attempt to heal ourselves through substances that will anethesize our feelings. We become unyielding in our pursuit of relationships. If I could just find the right man or woman, I will be whole. We meander from one place to another, trying whatever is convenient and whatever will get us through the next moment. Even our work becomes a means of healing ourselves, but at the end of our busy work day we come face to face with our brokenness again.

The determination to be healed is not enough. The woman with the issue of blood possessed that for 12 long years. She pursued her healing, but it was not until she came into the presence of Jesus that she was made whole. She reached out and touched the tassel of His garment. We certainly cannot physically touch Him, but we can come into His presence and be healed.

Our faith is what makes us whole, not our much doing and pursuing self-made remedies. Faith is to believe in the power of an unseen, but present God. Faith speaks to the ushering in of a new reality, even in the face of a long time condition of brokenness. Prayer is an act of faith that places us in the presence of God who will look through the portals of heaven, through the many who are pressing their way to Him, and say "who touched me?"

You need not continue to live in your brokenness. Come daily before the presence of God. Believe, by faith, that God is able to pick up the pieces. Release your mind from the hard work of trying to figure it out. Pray and leave the rest to God!!

WHAT BECOMES OF THE BROKENHEARTED?

Years ago a song was recorded entitled, "What Becomes Of The Brokenhearted?" To this day when I hear it, I experience a sense of incredible sadness. Jimmy Ruffin leaves you with the picture of someone who is doomed to wander through this landscape of life never finding a way to mend their broken heart. He laments about this condition by saying:

As I walk this land of broken dreams,
I have visions of many things,
But happiness is just an illusion,
Filled with heartache and confusion.

What becomes of the brokenhearted,
Who have loved and now departed,
I know I've got to find
some kind of peace of mind,
I've been searching everywhere,
Just to find someone to care.

The words leaves us with a lingering, sad melody and no answer to the question. Sadly enough, many people respond to their brokenness in the same way. They can identify the cause of the condition. They can get in touch with their feelings of discomfort, loneliness, abandonment, and despair. So many are never able to move beyond this point. The unspoken resolve is that brokenness is a permanent condition of life and that we are doomed to singing a sad song.

It wasn't until years later in my life that I found the answer to Jimmy Ruffin's question. I found it in the 34th Psalm. "The Lord is close to the brokenhearted and saves those who are crushed in spirit."

These words of the Psalmist leave us with a sense of hope, not despair. God specializes in healing the brokenhearted. We are told that He sent His son Jesus "to bind up the brokenhearted." The very presence of God provides us with our healing. We can only draw close to Him through prayer.

When you find yourself in a place of brokenness, don't sing a sad song, just pray. God is the ultimate source of all of our healing.

IN THE PURSUIT OF HEALING

Journey Thoughts

_____

_____

_____

_____

_____

_____

_____

_____

_____

August

A Resting Place

"Come with me by yourselves to a quiet
place and get some rest."

St. Mark 6:31b (NIV)

VIII. A Resting Place

Moments of Centering

Prayer

Dear God,

I am beginning to understand that rest is a necessary part of my spiritual journey and yet I feel guilty when I take some time to be renewed. This present age has taught me to be busy all the time. Teach me to re-order my way of thinking. I need to rest in your presence.

Journey Scriptures

Exodus 20:8-11
Psalm 46:1-10
Psalm 116:1-7
St. Mark 6:30-32
Hebrews 4:1-11

Journey Reflections

A Resting Place In God
Alone With God
Have You Rested Yet?
Be Still My Soul

Journal Writing

Write down your plans for a Sabbath day rest. Commit yourself to being true to what you have written.

Prayer

God, my soul longs to rest in you. I have been anxious about too many things and I have filled my days with too much work. Forgive me Lord. Now I know that my failure to rest is a sin. Thank you for teaching me to enjoy the blessings of "resting." Amen.

A Resting Place In God

The words of the Markan text arouses in us a longing to receive the invitation to rest, but it also stirs in us a degree of resistance. I suspect that we all dream of a place that is cleared of life's busyness; a place where we can lie down our tired souls and rest. And yet for those of us who are addicted to activities, we fear such a place. We equate the amount of continuous involvement or work that we do with our self-worth. We fear resting because our much doing is a way of supporting our sense of self and a security about who we are. In a subtle way, we somehow think that we were created to be "human doings" rather than "human beings." It is simply hard for us to rest. We are a driven people, which is an indication of our over-valuing ourselves and a lack of trust in God!

One day I decided to receive this invitation from Christ to rest. Initially, I resisted the small, yet persistent voice of Jesus calling me to go to a quiet place. I kept thinking I have so many things to do — agendas to plan, sermons to write, people to counsel, clothes to iron, groceries to buy — and on and on and on. Then I remembered that Jesus gave the invitation to the disciples, not after they had completed all the work, but while they were in the midst of it. And so I packed my bags, left all of the activity behind, and went to a place to rest.

The purpose of the invitation to rest is to give us an opportunity to refresh ourselves. Our resting allows us to quiet ourselves so that we can hear the words of God. When we rest we are not only more receptive to God, but to ourselves and others as well.

I'm glad that I accepted the invitation. As I sat quietly by the still waters, watching the colors on the horizon, and listening to the quiet voice of God — my soul was restored.

I have returned to the work (yes, it's still there), but having experienced the joy of rest, when Jesus bids me to "go away to a quiet place" again, I won't resist.

ALONE WITH GOD

The enemy of our spirit enjoys watching us continue to neglect the place of solitary prayer. We have been formed and fashioned by the ways of the world that instruct us to constantly engage in active works. We believe that the estimation of our value as a person is closely aligned with how much we accomplish. We are very impressed by our "success." As a matter of fact, we are addicted to them. So much so that we find ourselves unable to pull away from our "work" and spend some time in a quiet place.

This dilemma is experienced, not just in terms of our daily works, but it is also manifested in the work that we do in the church. Many are so involved in doing "God's" work, until they fail to take time to know the "God of the work." Knowing God does not come from choir rehearsals or ministry and organization meetings. What we do in God's church should be the outgrowth of what we have heard from God in prayer.

A church worker who does not take time to go to that solitary place of prayer can easily become destructive. This person begins to operate on personal feelings as opposed to divine direction. There is also the constant temptation of measuring the success of one's work by how much, and how often, one engages in it.

Jesus was not addicted to His ministry work nor was He impressed by how much He did or the results. He understood the danger of both and so he modeled for us the need to find that quiet center in our lives.

When we go to a solitary place, we can slowly unmask the illusion of ourselves and discover our real selves. In a solitary place we can discover that being is more important than doing and having, and that we are more important than the results of our efforts. When we get alone with God, we realize that our life is not a possession to be defended, but a gift to be shared.

When we are alone with God, we come to know that our worth is not the same as our usefulness.

Have You Rested Yet?

In God's economy there is a divine pattern of work and rest. The difficulty in our receiving God's invitation, or following his command to rest, is that we have been shaped by the tenets of Western theological thought. We have learned to think of God as pure activity and we often forget about the biblical references to God's resting. Thus, we associate our much activity with imagining God as one who never rests. After all, we are told that God never sleeps or slumbers. We are so caught up in the protestant work ethic until there is little awareness of the sacredness of rest. There is a tremendous amount of momentum in our lives that drives us and keeps us from resting. We feel inwardly compelled to stay busy all the time. It is simply hard for us to rest.

This obsession with our "much doing" is carried over into our prayer life. Prayer for most of us is not rest. Sometimes we come away from prayer more tired than when we entered it. Prayer becomes a place of rehearsing our agenda for the day: problem-solving, decision-making, or working out our future. Our time of praying is often just a continuation of the inner noise and struggle of our lives. The idea of prayer as a place of rest runs counter to the whole protestant work ethic. Prayer is often associated with doing nothing, and doing nothing makes us feel unproductive. It is painful for us to rest because resting means just sitting with things as they are for a while, just sitting with our unresolved struggles and anxieties, just sitting with our unattended worries and fears. In the silence of rest, we are forced to recognize our limitations and see all our underlying conflicts and bruised places to which we are blinding ourselves through the diversion of our busyness. There are so many forces and fears within us, pulling us away from a Sabbath resting in prayer, until we cannot afford to ignore the invitation.

This is the season of God bidding us to rest. The call to rest must be taken as seriously as the call to work. A tired, weary and worn believer is more vulnerable to the subtle tactics of the enemy than one who has been refreshed through resting. This journey includes rest stops along the way. Have You Rested Yet? If Not, Make The Decision To Do So Now!

BE STILL MY SOUL

In a world that is filled with noise, we find it difficult to embrace silence. As long as we listen to the sounds around us, we will not hear the voice within us. By divine design it is a still, small voice that does not scream to be heard, but waits in patient silence for us to incline an ear to it.

Actually, we think that it is virtually impossible to still our souls and hear that voice. The truth is, we are afraid to be quiet. Silence involves a risky surrender. It is a letting go of our need to be in control and stepping into a dimension where we are not sure of what we will hear. As long as we do all of the talking in our praying, we are in control. When we begin to cease the chatter we open ourselves to the risky business of hearing God, who we cannot manipulate into speaking what we want to hear.

Inner silence is the absence of any sort of inward stirring of thought or emotion. It is complete alertness and openness to God. Silence is the state in which all the powers of the soul and all the faculties of the body are completely at peace, quiet and recollected, alert, and free from any turmoil or agitation.

As long as our soul is not still, there can be no vision, and without a vision we perish. When we still our souls, we are brought in the very presence of God and we began to see more clearly. The enemy of our soul wants us to love the noise. If we stay addicted to it, we will never "hear" the vision for our lives. God has something to say to us that will be heard only in the stillness of the moment. Purpose is hidden in our souls; silence reveals it to us.

We need to practice the discipline of silence. Command your soul to be still. Take five minutes a day where you minimize the distractions, sit in quiet reflection, open yourself to God, and tell your soul to "be still." When you do so, you will experience the peace that passeth all understanding and you will begin to "hear" life from a different perspective.

A Resting Place

Journey Thoughts

_____

_____

_____

_____

_____

_____

_____

_____

_____

September

PRAYING THE VISION

"Where there is no vision, the people
perish:..."

Proverbs 29:18a (KJV)

IX. PRAYING THE VISION

Moments of Centering
Prayer

Dear God,

Good morning. Thank you for allowing me to see the dawn of a new day. As I approach this time of prayer, I come with a desire to see you. Give me clarity of focus and thought. Remove the veil from my eyes. There is a vision that I must see and Lord, when you reveal it to me, help me to be faithful to what I have seen.   Amen.

Journey Scriptures

Daniel 10:4-18
Isaiah 6:1-8
Habakkuk 2:1-3
Exodus 34:27-28
Revelation 1:1-10

Journey Reflections

Don't Perish - Pray
Prayer - The Place of Seeing
On Hearing The Vision
Write It Down

Journal Writing

The prophet Habakkuk says to you, "write the vision." Be obedient to the divine directive of the prophet.

Prayer for the Journey

Dear God,

I have seen the vision. Now God, give me the strength and the discipline to make it real.   Amen.

Don't Perish - Pray

If you want to see the vision for your life, you must practice the discipline of prayer. Without a vision, you perish. Without a prayer life, you have no vision.

To have vision means that you are able to see the "not yet" in your life, and even though it has not come to pass, you walk in the assurance that the vision will be made real. Those who have vision have direction and purpose. When you are able to see the plans for your life, you begin to eliminate anything that does not lead to the fulfillment of your purpose. That is why prayer is essential to those who want to live in the reality of vision.

Visions, plans, and purpose come from God. How can we know any of these if we do not pray. If we want to see clearly the direction of our lives, we must pray. In the place of prayer, God allows us to see the "not yet." In those moments of quiet communion with God, God places in our spirit that which has been ordained for us since we were in our mother's womb. Vision is revelation. Revelation comes only from God.

Prayer must be continuous, for God does not show us all of the vision at one time. We cannot pray today and expect to see all that God has for us. Each time we kneel to pray, God allows us to see another dimension of the vision. In prayer, God whispers to us those things we must do in order to make the vision real. God will let us see what we need to do, when we should start or stop, and who will help us as well as who will hinder us. Clarity of the vision only comes through prayer.

The quality of your prayer life will determine the quality of your vision for life. Pray without ceasing.

PRAYER - THE PLACE OF SEEING

There must be a place in our life for times of being alone with God. The vision for our lives will not be experienced in the midst of our being surrounded by people and things. Often we are mesmerized by, and addicted to, both. Only when we are willing to enter into solitude and uninterrupted communion with God will we be able to see the vision like Daniel.

Dwelling in a place of solitude does not come easily for us. We have a need to make decisions based upon the expectations and opinions of others. We are attached to "what others think" or "what others will say." While there are times when it is appropriate to be accountable to others and listen to them, we must know when it is time to release ourselves from their voices in order to hear the one who alone knows the way we must go.

Detachment and separation are requirements for those who want to enter into a new spiritual dimension. We cannot really commune with God and others at the same time. God refuses to compete and thus He bids us to move away to a quiet place where our attention can be fully focused on Him.

In the midst of the marketplace of His life, God instructed Daniel to go down to the banks of river Tigris. Daniel's obedience to that call allowed him to hear and see the vision. So often those of us who are engaged in God's work refuse to heed the call to solitude and consequently miss the vision. It was not easy for Daniel to leave the work of his prophetic office, for what he was doing was necessary and important; however, he somehow knew that in order to be more effective, he needed to receive some personal directions from God. In his alone time he was given a vision and the understanding of it. (Daniel alone saw the vision.)

Seasons of solitude are requirements for those who want to live a life that is guided by vision. Our alone times of prayer will free us from our bondage to people and our inner compulsions. They become moments of transformation, where we become more concerned about what God has to say and less concerned about the opinions of others.

The prayer of solitude sensitizes us to God. When God has our full attention, He begins to reveal to us the vision. It was on the banks of the river Tigris that Daniel saw the vision. The question becomes where will you go in order to see God's vision for your life?

ON HEARING THE VISION

When St. John the Divine was on the isle of Patmos, he saw and heard the vision. We are told that he was "in the spirit." To be in the spirit simply means to be in a place of prayer. Therefore, if we want to not only see the vision that God has for our life, but also to hear it, we must pray. There are, however, some prerequisites.

John was on the isle of Patmos. It was a solitary place. There he was removed from all distractions and interferences. He could give his attention fully and completely to God. In so doing, he experienced something unusual. Until we are like John and are able to have a singleness of focus and place ourselves in a position where nothing else holds our attention, we will not hear the voice of God.

An essential requirement for "hearing the vision" is being alone with God. This is why creating your own isle of Patmos is a requirement. There is merit in praying anywhere and at anytime; however, it is difficult to give your full attention to God in the midst of the activities of the marketplace of life. If we want to be "in the spirit" so that we can both "see and hear" the vision, then we must do as Jesus did and steal away to a solitary place.

Patmos was not a place of John's choosing. Actually, he was living in exile. It was not where he desired to live, but he understood that his prayer life would keep him during this difficult time. Often when we are in exile, we cease to pray. We tend to turn our attention from God to lamenting about our circumstances. Learning to pray in a strange land will catapult you into the presence of God.

In an unusual location, John found himself caught up in the spirit and he heard the voice of God as loud as a trumpet. There was no question, whether he knew that it was God. He was able to "hear the vision."

There are visions that God wants us to "hear", but the sound is muddled by our inattentiveness to our prayer life and to our willingness to go to Patmos. We will be able to hear God's voice and clearly receive directions for our vision if we simply learn to get alone and pray.

WRITE THE VISION

When I pray, I keep my journal by my side. As God speaks to me, I write it down. What God says does not always become an immediate reality. When my faith begins to waiver, I go back to my journal and re-read what God has shown me.

We like to talk, and occasionally we listen, but seldom do we write. My greatest struggle in putting this book of reflections together was the constant inner struggle of convincing myself that I could write. What I have come to accept and understand is that my ability to write is directly related to the quality of my prayer life. It was not until I committed myself to the discipline of prayer that I had anything worth writing.

During my prayer moments there were graced times in which God allowed me to see what eventually would come to pass - and I wrote it down. There have been times in which I have heard the voice of God - and I wrote it down. As I have communed with God, I have seen and heard. Often my mind is cluttered, my memory is short, my intentions not always realized, and details forgotten, so I have learned not to concentrate on my limited writing skills, but to simply write as the spirit of God gives me utterance.

If we believe that prayer is communicating with God, then we must know that God will speak to us and what God says is extremely important. A serious student never comes to class to hear the words of a learned professor without taking notes. Likewise, when we come before the one who has all knowledge and who speaks words of wisdom to us, we must be quick to write it down.

I suggest that you not place a yoke around your neck by having an unnecessary concern about how well you write, simply respond to what you have heard. Do not allow yourself to be in an unnecessary place of struggle. No, you will not hear God's voice or see the vision every time you kneel down to pray, but God will speak and when this happens — be ready to write. The prophet Habakkuk encourages us to write the vision and to make it plain for the vision is for an appointed time. As you wait for that appointed time, you will find comfort in reading what God has spoken to you.

Praying the Vision

Journey Thoughts

_____

_____

_____

_____

_____

_____

_____

_____

_____

October

A Dwelling Place

"Lord, you have been our dwelling place
throughout all generations."

Psalm 90:1 (NIV)

X. A Dwelling Place

Moments of Centering

Prayer

Dear God,

Prayer for me has been a quick in and out experience. The marketplace of my life beckons me to work and to be in perpetual motion. Teach me God how to sit a while with you. I commit myself to learning how to dwell in your presence. Amen.

Journey Scriptures	Journey Reflections
Psalm 63	Can You Stay Awhile?
Psalm 90	It Is No Secret
Psalm 91	Staying Close to God's Side
Psalm 84	Longing To Be There
Psalm 73	

Journal Writing

Write as the Psalmist would, expressing the way that you have found a dwelling place in God's presence.

Prayer for the Journey

Dear God,

A dwelling place is necessary for my life. Even when I didn't know to abide with you for awhile, you were there with me. Now I know and I will stay. Amen.

Can You Stay Awhile?

I grew up with the image of a father who spent a significant amount of time on his knees. My father prayed for a long time. As a child I used to think "What is he doing? Does he really have that much to say to God? Does it take all of that?" I no longer ask these questions, because now I know. He stayed there awhile because prayer was my father's dwelling place.

To dwell is to stay for awhile, to settle down, to sink into, to become immersed in, to be still and focused. To dwell in the presence of God, simply means to be present to God for a significant amount of time. In a world that teaches us to always be on the go, we have become dulled to the discipline of staying put. Our natural inclination is to move quickly from one experience to another and to flee quickly from that which does not yield immediate results. Dwelling is not a natural part of our world's reality.

The spiritual malaise that affects so many Christians is our inability to spend time in the presence of God. Our "dis-ease" causes us to either avoid that time of staying on bended knees or if we do so, we have self-imposed time constraints. Consequently, we seldom really experience the joy of dwelling in God's presence.

My father died a few years ago. The week of his death we talked every day. He was preparing to do a workshop on meditation. His excitement was uncontainable. Daddy called me on Friday and said, "the Holy Spirit has given me the scripture to use. It is Psalm 91:1." The next day, in the midst of his workshop presentation while expounding on this scripture, I am told that he looked upward, gently slumped to the floor, and died. My mother says that he had the glory of God all over his face.

When we learned to stay a while with God, we will receive a peace which passeth all understanding. I promise you that I never saw my father worry about anything.   Because he spent time with God, he had the assurance of God's presence and the confidence of knowing that no matter what happened, he would rest in the shadow of God.

It Is No Secret

It really is no secret what God can do! The knowledge of God's ability to do the impossible in our lives is directly related to the quality of our prayer life. Prayer is the place where God reveals His "secret" thoughts to us. We will not know the hidden things of God until we are willing to dwell in God's presence - or until we learn to pray.

Many will say they pray, but in actuality they only occasionally approach God. Oh, they conjure up one or two fleeting acts of hope in Him, but there is no commitment to consistency and longevity. They do not habitually reside in God's mysterious presence.

The secret place of God is the Holy of Holiest. Not every one enters therein, only those who have received Jesus Christ, whose death gave us access to this special place. We come to it by entering our inner sanctuary, where our ultimate interest is to commune with God. It is a place reserved for those who are able to receive the love of God, want to walk in obedience to his son Jesus, and need to be empowered by the Holy Spirit.

When we pray we are establishing intimacy with God. Intimacy implies an unusual closeness. It is a sense of shared privacy. It is unrestrained communion and an act of trust. Our acts of prayer say that we have confidence in God. Our willingness to spend uninterrupted moments with God is an indication of our level of confidence in Him. We don't mind staying in the presence of the one to whom we can tell all things without fear of being violated.

So in prayer we learn to rest and to be at peace. There we lodge quietly and securely.

No, it is no secret to the one who dwells in God's presence what God can do. To them the veil is rent, the mercy seat is revealed, the hovering cherubs are manifest, and the glory of the Most High God is apparent. The one who prays comes away with heavenly information known only to the angels. They come away with a new way of seeing and perceiving the things of this world. No longer are they tossed to and fro, easily disturbed, and filled with anxiety. Through prayer, they now know the secret of what God can do!

STAYING CLOSE TO GOD SIDE

A few years ago while I was attending a revival, I heard a minister give an illustration that has remained with me through the years. Rev. Salter was speaking from the 91st Psalm and wanted his audience to see vividly the blessings that come when we stay close to God. When Rev. Salter was a young boy, he and several of his cousins would go and spend the summer with his grandmother. Like many grandmothers of that day, she was known for her culinary abilities, in particular her baking. Often while she was in the kitchen stirring up a cake, all of the children except Rev. Salter, would go outside to play. She kept an eye on them as she prepared one of their favorite desserts. Usually they stayed outside for a long time, never bothering to check with grandma. Rev. Salter, however, stayed right by her side and in so doing, every now and then she would allow him to taste the batter from the cake. When the cake was baked all of the children had a piece, but the one who stayed close to grandma had received the privilege of a foretaste.

Certainly God loves all of His children and keeps a watchful eye on each one. For those who stay close by God's side, however, he gives a foretaste of

His blessings.

When we create a dwelling place, a place of prayer, we become a part of God's inner circle and thus the recipient of some special blessings. In prayer, as we stay close to God's side, God reaches down and gives to us what those who stay far from Him will never receive. Staying close to God puts us in a position to receive the secret things of God.

The Psalmist tells us that if we dwell in the secret place of God, there are some benefits that we receive. First of all, there we will find rest. When we pray, we eventually come to know that God can take care of us and so beneath the wings of God's love we allow ourselves to abide. Secondly, we learn that God is our refuge and therefore we need not fear anyone or anything. The more we commune with God, the more we are aware of His awesome power. Third, staying in close proximity to God shortens the distance that the angels have to travel to us. He will command His angels to guard us in all our ways.

Go to your dwelling place each day and receive those special blessings that are reserved for those who stay close to God's side.

LONGING TO BE THERE

Have you ever experienced an inner longing? Have you ever tried to satisfy that longing only to find that it was still there? The truth is we have misinterpreted the nature of this inner discontent. It cannot be satisfied through the seeking of some external remedy. This restlessness has been placed in us by God. This inward rumbling is an indication of our spirit's desire to be in the presence of God.

The words of the 84th Psalm express the joy that is experienced when we come to the awareness of what our soul needs - a divine dwelling place. The temple assistant who wrote this Psalm was going through a difficult time in his life; however, because he had already established a relationship with God, he knew that he could find no peace until he came into the courts of God.

During seasons of turbulence, we often do not understand what we really need. Our solutions only increase the agitation. The Psalmist, however, recognized that no matter what crisis was in his life, ultimately the problem was an internal one. He says, "my soul yearns, even faints, for the courts of the Lord." Longing in the Hebrew means to be consumed with, or in the Latin- "deperire alique amore" - dying of love. This is a longing whose desire is so great until one will waste and pine away unless his/her wish is gratified. It is an ardent longing, which so torments and burns the mind until the flesh and marrow waste away, so long as it is not permitted to enjoy the thing that it desires. "My soul yearns even faints for the courts of the Lord."

The satisfaction to our longings is found only in God's dwelling place. Only there do we find a source of relief for our yearning. Our souls are made to rest and the inner turbulence subsides. If a sparrow can find a home for herself on God's altar, can't we? Our strength comes from being in the presence of God.

Do you long to be there? Do you have that yearning, an intense desire to be with God? Have you come to the realization that no matter what the situation, ultimately the place of your satisfaction is the courts of the Lord? If so, the Psalmist declare that you will be richly blessed and go from strength to strength.

A Dwelling Place

<u>Journey Thoughts</u>

_____

_____

_____

_____

_____

_____

_____

_____

November

THEY THAT WAIT

"But they that wait on the Lord shall
renew their strength; they shall mount
up on wings as eagles; they shall run, and
not be weary; and they shall walk, and
not faint."

Isaiah 40:31 (KJV)

XI. They That Wait

Moments of Centering

Prayer

Dear God,

Your ways are not like my ways. Teach me how to wait on you and to trust what you are doing even when I can't see or feel anything. Transform me into the patient person that you would have me to become. Today as I pray, as I sing, and as I play, I wait with anticipation and expectation for you. Amen.

Journey Scriptures	Journey Reflections
Isaiah 40:27-31	They That Wait
Daniel 10:1-14	A Cosmic Delay
Hebrews 10:32-39	While You Wait
Jude 1:17-24	We Have Need of Patience

Journal Writing

Something should happen in us while we wait for God. Write about your waiting experience.

Prayer for the Journey

Dear God,

Thank you for teaching me how to wait. Amen.

A Cosmic Delay

I remind you to not be discouraged when you do not receive an immediate answer or manifestation of the answer to your prayers. There is a cosmic delay - the time between the prayer and the prayer answered. *From the first day that you set your mind to gain understanding and to humble yourself before God, your words are heard. (Daniel 10:12)* It is precisely your posture in prayer that may cause the delay. Daniel came before God with a contrite heart, a spirit of repentance and a total dependency on God. His prayer stance enabled his prayers to "touch heaven." Arrogance, independence, and failure to confess our sins are a hinderance to our being able to "get a prayer through." When we humble ourselves, strip away the pretense and open our mind, heart and spirit to God with the intent of seeking divine understanding, then from the moment that we pray, God hears!

......But the prince of the Persian Kingdom resisted me for 21 days. (Daniel 10:13)

The cosmic struggle has begun! Although Daniel had prayed the "right way", he had to wait 21 days for the answer. Why? Because from the very moment of his praying, the ruler of the prince of the air went into action and spiritual warfare began. Gabriel had been dispatched to give the answer, but the prince of Persia detained him. Thus, Daniel had the wait for the answer.

We too experience delayed responses to our "most sincere and humble" prayers. Instead of becoming discouraged (which is what the evil spirit wants us to do), it would be instructive for us to remember that there are principalities and rulers of the darkness. The "prince of Persia" assign one of his "imps" to war against our angelic messenger, thus delaying the response to our prayers. The ultimate intent is to have us to get tired of the waiting and to give up, to stop praying!

......Then Michael came to help me (Daniel 10:13).

The cosmic delay does not last forever. Be encouraged. Keep praying and don't lose hope while you wait. Help is on the way!

WHILE YOU WAIT

What is it that you desire more, the thing for which you have prayed or to be in the presence of the one to whom you are praying? If it is the first, then our waiting becomes a time of anxiety, frustration, and discouragement. If it is the latter, our strength is renewed and we will be able to mount up on wings like an eagle.

The ultimate purpose of our praying has to extend far beyond our being fulfilled through the receiving of the answer to our prayers. It is true that God wants us to have the desires of our heart, but sometimes we become fixated and preoccupied with what we want. Thus, what becomes priority is not our praying, but our receiving. And when we do not "receive" that for which we have prayed, we begin to question God, wonder what we did wrong and eventually see ourselves as being ostracized from God's inner circle of blessings. I suspect that God permits us "to wait" for the answer to our prayers to test our hearts. If your heart's desire is to be in relationship with God, then our waiting becomes a time of joy, not a season of despair.

Waiting on God is not a place of inactivity, instead it is a "getting busy" with God. They that wait, are those who spend quality time seeking more of God. They are not "stuck" on whether or not they receive that for which they have prayed. Instead, the waiting becomes a time in which we learn to enjoy being in God's presence. Our place of prayer is our waiting station. There we sink into the comfort of God's bosom and allow ourselves to be covered by God's wings. We do not flee from God's presence, but each day we run to it. And although we asked, because we wanted that for which we prayed, somehow it is no longer an obsession for us. We begin to desire more of God and less of "things."

While you wait, spend quality time with God. Think and reflect on God's goodness, and God's attributes. Allow God's glory to fill your prayer space. You will find that your strength will be renewed and your heart is content. Don't stop waiting!

WE HAVE NEED OF PATIENCE

We are the product of our time. We live in an age of acceleration, in an era so seduced by the instantaneous that we are in danger of losing our ability to wait. This life moves at an amazing pace. Computers yield up immediate answers. Pictures develop before your eyes. Satellites beam television signals from practically anywhere, allowing far away images to appear right in our living rooms. Space travel, fax machines, and e-mail; we are encapsulated in a speeding world.

It is inevitable that the lure of the quick and easy would slip into our spiritual life. We find ourselves wanting instantaneous results on this prayer journey. When we pray, we are impatient. God, however, is not moved by our need to have quick and easy results to our prayers. The ultimate aim of prayer is for a deep change to take place in our personality, in our inner being. Such a re-creation does not happen spontaneously or without effort and pain. We do have need of patience.

Our waiting should become a time in which we emerge into something new. When we commune with God, we do so not just to receive another "gadget in our lives" or to make our living easy. We are in touch with God so that we might become transformed. He that has begun a good work in us is committed to its completion. It takes time for us to separate ourselves from our addiction to things and people. Transformation cannot occur without separation. We are an "attached" people. Our understanding of who we are is so interwoven into our possessions that the notion of loosening ourselves from them frightens us. We rebel against it. We loosely use the phrase "let go and let God," but the truth is we want to "hold on and manipulate God!" Prayer is an experience of growth of maturity in the faith. Waiting is a part of that process. We are given time to look at those attachments, see our addiction to them, and begin to separate ourselves. It is a difficult process. We must be patient.

When we come to understand the nature of our waiting, then we become patient. Wait, work, detach, and transform are the operative words of the one who prays. To pray in this manner places us in the will of God, and allows us to receive the promise.

THEY THAT WAIT

When we engage in the experience of prayer, we know that we are doing that which is good and pleasing unto God. Somewhere in the recesses of our mind we also know that our act of prayer will ultimately benefit us. The truth is that though we intellectually know that it is "all good," sometimes we do grow weary in our praying because the answers do not come as quickly as we desire.

I had an occasion to do a workshop on prayer. I asked each person to write down a word that would best describe their prayer life. In the time of sharing, I heard words like, "stale, inconsistent, non-existent, dry, pitiful, and tired." As we engaged in further conversation, I heard many express their disappointment in prayer. Most had seemingly grown weary because they had not received certain anticipated responses from God. They prayed, but had moments when they felt as though they were not being heard.

Prayer is not an experience of receiving immediate results. More often than not, prayer is an experience of struggling and waiting. When we pray we sometimes feel as though we are lost in a myriad of unanswered requests. We stumble through trying to find the right words and feeling embarrassed before God when we can't. There are moments in which our petitions seem to bounce off the ceiling and ricochet back to us. We get up from our knees in a state of confusion. And yes, we do get weary in our praying.

Being weary in prayer is a dangerous place to reside. If we stay there for too long, we will begin to disconnect from God. Without speaking it, in covert ways we begin to allow doubt and disbelief to creep into our heart, mind, and spirit. Bit by bit we decrease our time of praying. When we allow this to happen, the hearing of the voice of God decreases and the voice of the enemy of our existence grows louder. The order of the spiritual life is that of patient waiting. God has so ordained and divinely designed prayer to be a waiting station. Instant responses and immediate satisfaction are the things of this world — that which comes from God cannot be confined to our time schedule.

Ultimately, we who pray must elevate our trust in God and continue to pray, for in due season we shall reap the benefits of our praying, if we faint not.

They That Wait

_____

_____

_____

_____

_____

_____

_____

_____

December

THE JOURNEY HOME

"I will set out and go back to my father....."

St. Luke 15:18a (NIV)

XII. THE JOURNEY HOME

Moments of Centering

Prayer

Dear God,

Long ago you gave to me a home in your son Jesus Christ. Help me to return to Him fully and completely. I have strayed and now I know that I must return. I offer my life as a home to you, and ask for your grace and strength to live as your child.

Journey Scriptures

Exodus 3:11-15
Jeremiah 29:10-14
Psalm 139:1-18
St. Matthew 6:28-33
St. Luke 15:11-24

Journey Reflections

Who Am I?
What Do I Want?
How Will I Get What I Want?
Make Room For Jesus

Journey Writing

Write a letter to God, letting Him know how you desire to stay at home with Him.

Closing Prayer for the Journey

Dear God,

As I face the end of another year, my heart is filled with praise. I have found my home in you. I know who I am, my purpose and how to receive what you have for me. Holy Spirit, keep me in the path that leads me home. Amen.

WHO AM I ?

The late theologian Howard Thurman, was able to capture the essence of our existence when he stated that basically there are three questions that confronts us in life — "Who Am I? What Do I Want? and How Do I Propose To Get It?" The quality of life is determined by the way in which we choose to answer these questions. The latter two questions cannot be answered with any accuracy until we are able to respond to the first.

The lack of self knowledge is the primary contributing entity for our confusion. We have allowed our identity to be shaped by other than self-definitions. Although we are told not to be conformed to this world, the reality is, we are so entrenched in the "things of this world" that they become the means by which we define ourselves. Our reality changes based upon the minds of politicians, the whims of the business world, and the schemes of the entertainment industry. The problem with using those means of establishing our identity lies in the instability of all the aforementioned. They change based upon personal greed and self-aggrandizement. So, when we come to the conclusion as to who we are based upon the dictates of our existential reality, we really don't know who we are.

Take away our jobs, degrees, plaques, accomplishments, retirement gifts, children, spouses, relationships, positions in the church or in the community; take away our material possessions, American made or foreign cars, designer clothes, c.d's, vcr's, time-sharing, and credit cards — and we will not know who we are. Take away our complaints, murmuring, nursing of our pain, getting attention by always lifting up our problems; take away our need to be needed, our being comfortable with being down all the time — and we will not know who we are.

Howard Thurman has also stated that within each of us is a place called "the homing instinct." It is the divine longing to find one's self. Thurman's theological anthropology says to us, "within us is the spirit of God. God's spirit searches for identity - for our sake. That identity can only be established when we make the inward journey home to God.

Uncover who you really are and make the journey home. Your identity is wrapped in a manger, hidden from the cruel trappings of the world, but exposed to the divine presence of God. The one in the manger is the one who can take you home to his Father — who ultimately tells us who we are!

WHAT DO I WANT ?

At the core of life is a hard purposefulness, a determination to live. There is something irresistible about the methodical way life pounces upon whatever may be capable of sustaining it and will not release it until its own sustenance is guaranteed or fulfilled. It is a natural, fundamental characteristic of life — the innate search for nourishment or satisfaction. Life seeks to fulfill itself, that is to "live itself out." The point is that life, wherever it is found, is trying to live itself out or actualize its unique potential. In other words, the very essence of our lives requires an answer to the question "What Do I Want?" How we answer this query determines the quality of our lives.

The pursuit of the answer is not foreign to any of us. We have tried to find the response by focusing on things that are external and tangible. With rugged determination we have pursued our wants only to discover that the void, the emptiness, is still with us. So we devise another plan, conjure up another set of goals, and dream yet another dream. We face a rude awakening when we are confronted with truth — much of what we want is against life and what is against life is ultimately against God. The question then becomes not what do I want, but what does God want for my life. There is a paradox in operation here — in order to receive our wants we must be willing to surrender.

To surrender is to yield the nerve center of your consent to God. This is what we were born to do — it is our sovereign right and birthright privilege. When we yield the center of our being to God, and exchange our desires for God's, we experience for the first time a sense of coming home. Attempts to answer life's basic question apart from God places us in a strange land.

The story of the prodigal son illustrates the point. This young man had the need to find a response to life's question. He thought the answer was in a place different from his home. After receiving what he thought he wanted, he discovered that he was in a foreign place. The scriptures state that when he came to himself, he went home to his father.

This season of Christmas is about our making the journey home to God. God, in His infinite wisdom, knows that apart from our relations to him, we cannot satisfy our wants. God has provided the opportunity for us to answer one of the most fundamental questions of life. He did so by sending His son Jesus to us. No longer must we seek that which does not satisfy. We have an answer in Jesus!

How Will I Get What I Want

Advent is a season of waiting, but waiting is not a discipline that we have learned to embrace. Like the children of Israel, we want it when we want it! God had promised Israel that the Savior would come, but Israel did not know how to wait and took matters into their own hands. They devised plans, came up with devious schemes, engaged in less than noble behavior, and implemented their own proposals to get what they wanted. They looked to other "gods" and consistently forgot that God had a divine plan for their lives. They did not know how to "wait" on God.

When we are unable to wait, we devise our own plans and move outside of the realm of dependency on God. Self-made life proposals indicate a lack of trust and faith in God and eventually leads to a place of misery and despair. All of us have attempted to answer the question "how do I propose to get what I want?" (Remember I have said there are three questions we struggle to answer: who am I?, what do I want?, and how do I propose to get it?). Unfortunately, we are all guilty of trying to receive an answer without waiting on God. We have designed, planned, and implemented our own proposals!

Our proposals have included dressing for success, networking (using people to get what we want), positioning ourselves to be in the "right place at the right time", climbing the corporate ladder, (and being determined to be the one who breaks the glass ceiling), obtaining yet another degree, moving to the best neighborhood, marrying the best catch, investing our money for the future, and working longer and harder than anyone else. We find ourselves engaging in covert tragedy and overt behavior that is less than honest, manipulative, and somewhat devious. The tragedy of it all is that self-made proposals leave us looking for an answer.

Christmas is about the manifestation of God's proposal for us. God's plan for us is good and perfect. These words are recorded in Jeremiah 29:11, "For I know the plans I have for you," declares the Lord, "plans to prosper you and not to harm you, plans to give you hope and a future." How should we propose to get what we want? I suggest that we learn how to wait on God!

Making Room For Jesus

It is true that our lives are surrounded with so much movement, so many pressures, and so many demands that our spirits are often crowded into a corner. As soon as we awake in the morning, we are taken over by the ruthlessness of our daily routine. Once out of bed, our daily planners take over (Franklin or Covey). In some ways this is good. It means that there is a regularity and a structure to our days that make it possible for us to accomplish tasks that would be otherwise impossible.

There is however, another aspect to the matter of daily schedules, an oppressive aspect. Often we allow ourselves to become prisoners to our agendas. We become busy (note the words), not we are busy, but we become busy. Within ourselves we develop an inner sense of rushing. The danger is that while we might accomplish much and we are able to cross out all the things we have completed at the end of the day, the reality is that our spirits are crowded by our much doing.

We are entering into a season of much busyness. In addition to what we are already doing, we begin now to write in our planner all of the shopping, cooking, and festivities of the Christmas season. The joy and the peace of this time eludes us as we frantically run from store to store and event to event trying to get ready for Christmas. Ironically, when the day comes, we miss the visitation of the Christ Child for there was no room for His coming in our schedule.

We must decide to make room for Jesus. Advent is a season of preparation for His coming. We should cross out some of our things to do and write in time for Jesus. Make room for Him, by not doing so much on Saturday until you are too tired to worship Him on Sunday. Instead of reading all of the newspaper and every popular magazine, take time to read His word. Make room for Jesus — seek to do the will of God in your life. Make room for Jesus — start every morning by spending 20 minutes of quiet time with Him (or each night). Make room for Jesus — and let Him abide in your life.

The Journey Home

Journey Thoughts

_____

_____

_____

_____

_____

_____

_____

_____

_____